CHRISTOPHER
The Holy Giant

CHRISTOPHER
The Holy Giant

Tomie dePaola

Holiday House/New York

FOR
Father Dick Lower,
Father Omer Dufault,
and Rosli Hanslin,
who are all true "Christophers."

T. deP.
New Hampshire

Library of Congress Cataloging-in-Publication Data
De Paola, Tomie.
Christopher : the holy giant / by Tomie dePaola. — 1st ed.
p.   cm.
Summary: As Reprobus carries a child across a river one
stormy night, the boy gets heavier and heavier until Reprobus
feels he is carrying the world on his shoulders—thus goes
the legend of the name Christ-bearer, or Christopher.
ISBN 0-8234-0862-0
1. Christopher, Saint—Juvenile literature.   [1. Christopher,
Saint.   2. Saints.]   I. Title.
BX4700.C57D4   1994   90-49926   CIP   AC
398.22—dc20
[92]
ISBN 0-8234-1169-9 (pbk.)

A long time ago, in the land of Canaan, there lived a giant known as Reprobus. Because he was so big and strong, Reprobus wished to serve the greatest and most powerful king in all the world. So he set off to find him.

Before long, he came to a glorious city.
"Who is the ruler of this place?" Reprobus asked.
"The greatest king in all the world," the people answered.

"Then it is he I wish to serve," said Reprobus.
And he did.

One night, a minstrel sang before the court, and in his song, the name of the devil was mentioned again and again.

Every time the king heard the devil's name, he made the sign of the cross.

"O Mighty King," said Reprobus, "why do you do this?"

"I fear the devil and his power over me," the king answered. "I cross myself so that he won't harm me."

If the king fears the devil, then the devil must be greater and more powerful than he, said Reprobus to himself. I shall go and seek this devil and ask if I can serve him.

Reprobus traveled for many months until he came to the edge of a vast desert. And there he met a fearsome creature.
"Where are you going?" asked the creature.

"I am looking for the devil," Reprobus answered, "because I have heard he is the mightiest of all, and I wish to serve him."

"Then come with me. I *am* the devil," said the creature.

As Reprobus and the creature set off, they came upon a cross high on a hillside. The devil shook with fear and hid his face.

"We must turn back," he said.

"Why are you afraid?" asked Reprobus.

"The cross belongs to Christ, who is even more powerful than I am," said the devil.
"Then I shall seek this Christ and serve him," said Reprobus.

So he wandered across the dry desert until he came upon an old hermit who lived there.

"Do you know of a great king called Christ?" Reprobus asked.

The holy man smiled gently and began to talk about Jesus Christ. "He is the son of God and the greatest king of all," he said.

"Tell me how to find him, so I can serve him," said Reprobus.

"You cannot find *him*," the hermit said. "You must pray, and Christ will find *you*."

"But I don't know how to pray," Reprobus said.

"Stay with me and I will teach you," said the hermit. "Then you will be told how best to serve Christ."

One morning, the hermit said to Reprobus, "On the other side of the desert is a mighty river. Many have perished trying to cross. Go there.

Because you are so strong and tall, carry all who ask to the other side. Then I am sure Christ will reveal himself to you."

And Reprobus went. He built himself a hut beside the fast-flowing

river and carried many people across on his strong shoulders.

One stormy night while he slept, Reprobus heard the voice of a child calling, "Come, Reprobus, and carry me over."

He looked out into the dark and saw no one.

"It must have been the wind," Reprobus said to himself. Again he heard the voice and again he saw no one. The third time that the voice called, he went out and there on the banks of the river stood a child.

"Reprobus, carry me across the river," the child said.
So Reprobus lifted the child onto his shoulders, took his staff,
and started to wade through the stormy waters.

The river began to rise, the water churned, and the current grew stronger and stronger. As Reprobus struggled to cross, the child on his shoulders seemed to grow heavier.

The further he went, the higher the water rose and the heavier the child became. But Reprobus pushed on, even though he feared he might drown in the storm.

At last, Reprobus reached the other side of the river, and he set the child down.

"You put me in great danger, child," he said. "You were so heavy that I felt I was carrying the whole world on my shoulders."

"Reprobus," the child said, "not only were you carrying the world, you were carrying the son of Him who created it. I am Jesus Christ, the king whom you have been serving by this river. From now on, you shall be known as Christopher—Bearer-of-Christ.

"And to show that you serve me, set your staff in the ground next to your hut. Tomorrow you shall see it flower and bear fruit."

At that, the child vanished and Christopher did as he was told. The next morning, there in front of the hut, Christopher found his staff sprouting leaves and flowers and bearing dates, just as the child said it would.

From that day on, Christopher lived a holy life. He became the patron saint of travelers and his image was placed in many churches. People would go and pray before his image and say, "Behold Saint Christopher. Go thy way in safety."

Author's Note

The great spiritual writer, Caryll Houselander (1901–1954), believed that the stories of the saints rivaled many well-known fairy tales in their beauty and appeal for children. Among the most beautiful of these stories is the legend of St. Christopher. Probably no saint captured the imagination and attention of people more than Christopher, the Patron of Travel.

When I was growing up, the first thing we put on the dashboard of a new family car was not "fuzzy dice," but a St. Christopher medal. In fact, even our non-Catholic friends wouldn't think of getting on an airplane without a St. Christopher medal in their pockets. In 1969, in an effort to reorganize the liturgical year and a new calendar, the Catholic Church removed St. Christopher from the Calendar of the Saints. There was a question of whether or not he historically existed. So, the lovely story of the giant Reprobus and how he became known as Christopher was suddenly not available to children—at least not in Sunday schools.

The image of the giant carrying the Christ Child across the stormy river is one of the most stirring images in classical church art. My favorite is a fresco on a column in the Basilica of San Petronius in Bologna, Italy. One does not notice the fresco at first. It is a lovely surprise. So, whether Christopher did or did not exist does not concern me. I just want this legend and its accompanying imagery to be available again to all children.

T. deP.
New Hampshire